From Seed to Apple Tree

Following the Life Cycle

by
Suzanne Slade

illustrated by
Jeff Yesh

PICTURE WINDOW BOOKS
Minneapolis, Minnesota

Thanks to our advisers for their expertise, research, and advice:

Kathryn Orvis, Ph.D., Associate Professor/Extension Specialist
Department of Youth Development & Agricultural Education
Purdue University, West Lafayette, Indiana

Terry Flaherty, Ph.D., Professor of English
Minnesota State University, Mankato

Editor: Shelly Lyons
Designer: Lori Bye
Page Production: Melissa Kes
Art Director: Nathan Gassman
Editorial Director: Nick Healy
The illustrations in this book were created digitally.

Picture Window Books
151 Good Counsel Drive
P.O. Box 669
Mankato, MN 56002-0669
877-845-8392
www.picturewindowbooks.com

Photo Credits: Getty Images/StockFood Creative/Schnare & Stief, 23.

Printed in the United States of America.

 All books published by Picture Window Books
are manufactured with paper containing at least
10 percent post-consumer waste.

Library of Congress Cataloging-in-Publication Data
Slade, Suzanne.
From seed to apple tree : following the life cycle / by Suzanne Slade ;
illustrated by Jeff Yesh.
p. cm. — (Amazing Science: Life Cycle)
Includes index.
ISBN 978-1-4048-5159-7 (library binding)
1. Apples—Life cycles—Juvenile literature. I. Yesh, Jeff, 1971- ill. II. Title.
SB363.S57 2009
634'.11—dc22   2008037903

Table of Contents

Amazing Apple Trees

Apples are a delicious, nutritious fruit that people around the world enjoy eating. There are thousands of different kinds of apple trees. Each kind of apple tree grows fruit that has its own size, color, and taste. All full-size apple trees have the same basic life cycle. Let's follow the life cycle of a Golden Delicious apple tree.

Apple trees come in three basic sizes. There are full-size, semi-dwarf, and dwarf apple trees. Many orchard growers raise semi-dwarf or dwarf trees, because those trees grow fruit at a younger age than full-size trees.

Small Beginnings

The life of an apple tree begins with a small, brown seed. The seed comes from the core of the apple. An apple seed is about the size of a grain of rice. Rain helps the tiny seed begin to grow.

seed

Once planted, an apple seed grows roots. These roots grow downward and pull in water from the soil. Next, a shoot forms and pushes upward through the ground. It grows tall as it reaches for the warm sunlight.

shoot

roots

When people plant an apple tree, they usually plant it as a seedling. Apple trees need lots of sun, so they are not planted where they will be shaded by other trees.

Seedling to Sapling

Soon, soft green leaves appear on the shoot. The shoot becomes a seedling. Within about two years, this small plant becomes a young apple tree called a sapling. The sapling is stronger than the seedling, and its trunk is thicker too.

seedling

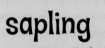

sapling

An apple tree uses water, sunlight, and air to make its own food. This process is called photosynthesis. Photosynthesis happens within the leaves of a tree.

Changes Throughout the Seasons

An apple tree grows and changes throughout the seasons. In early spring, small bumps called leaf buds appear. After these buds turn into leaves, the tree begins to make and store food. It grows all summer long.

spring

summer

When cold temperatures arrive in fall, the tree's leaves change color and fall off. During winter, the apple tree stays alive by using the food it stored during summer.

fall

winter

Apple trees need several weeks of low temperatures each year. The low temperatures are needed to help the plant to flower. Warmer weather in spring makes the tree bloom.

Full Grown

When a Golden Delicious apple tree is about 5 to 7 years old, it is considered an adult tree. An adult tree reaches a height of around 30 feet (9.2 meters). Each year in spring, an adult tree grows flower buds.

Apples trees are part of the rose family. Apple blossoms are white and pink and look like roses that grow in the wild.

Pollination

In the middle of April, an apple tree's pink buds open into flowers called blossoms. The stamens, or male parts of a blossom, make a liquid called nectar. Bees and other insects sip nectar from apple blossoms. When a bee takes in nectar, yellow dust called pollen sticks to its body. Pieces of pollen dust often fall off the bee when the bee visits another blossom.

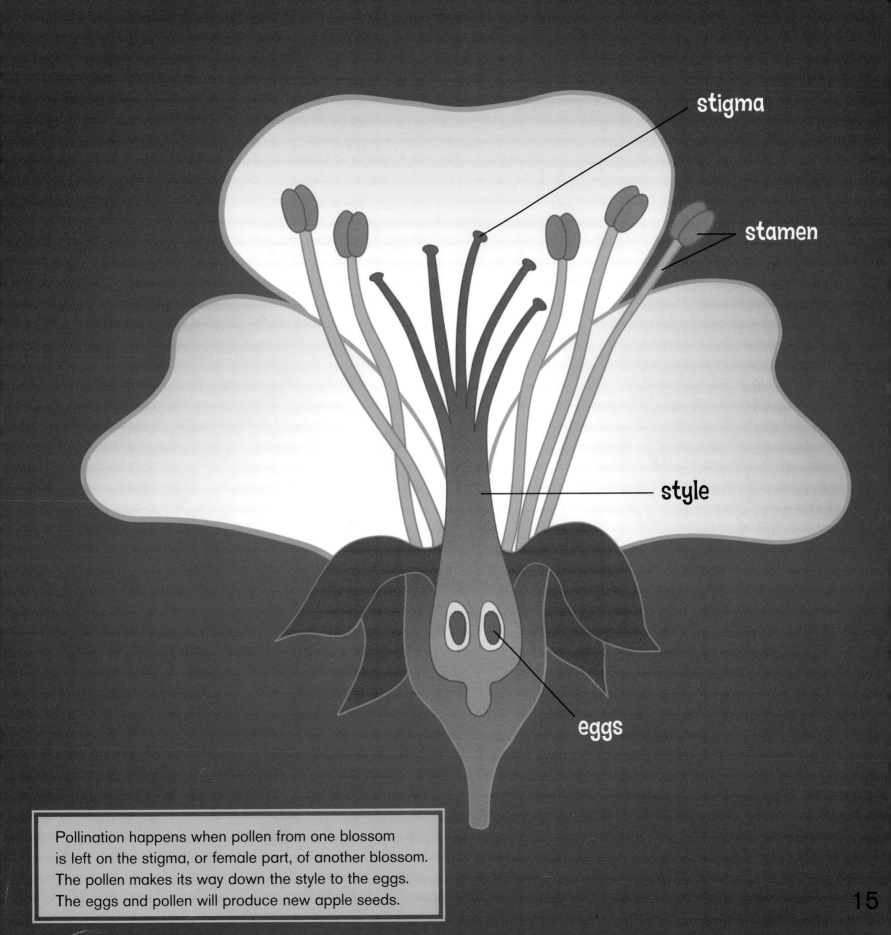

stigma

stamen

style

eggs

Pollination happens when pollen from one blossom
is left on the stigma, or female part, of another blossom.
The pollen makes its way down the style to the eggs.
The eggs and pollen will produce new apple seeds.

Tiny Apples

In early May, blossom petals begin to dry up and fall off. A few weeks later, a small bump starts to grow where the blossom had been. This tiny bump is a new apple.

Blossoms smell sweet and are brightly colored to attract bees and other insects. After a blossom is pollinated, its petals fall off, because it no longer needs insects to bring pollen.

Growing Big

A new apple gets sugar and water from the tree to help it grow. As it gets bigger, it also becomes round. This small, sour apple keeps growing throughout the hot summer months.

Golden Delicious apples change from dark green to light yellow as they grow larger. The larger apples often have a bit of pink on the skin.

Harvest Time

In October, the apples on a Golden Delicious apple tree turn yellow. The apples are sweet on the inside. They are ripe and ready to eat.

In the wild, apples fall to the ground, and life cycles of new Golden Delicious apple trees will begin.

An apple tree can live as long as 100 years.
As the tree gets older, it produces less fruit.

Life Cycle of a Golden Delicious Apple Tree

4. Adult tree
(5-100 years)

1. Seed
(5-6 months)

2. Seedling
(1 year)

3. Sapling
(2-5 years)

Fun Facts

- The average American eats about 65 apples per year. Golden Delicious apples are the third-most popular apples in the United States.

- It takes about 36 apples to get enough juice to make 1 gallon (3.8 liters) of apple cider.

- Apple farmers plant new trees by grafting. They cut off a branch from an adult tree and join it to a young apple tree. The branch and young tree will grow together to form a new tree. The new tree will produce the same kind of apples as the tree from which the branch was originally cut.

Golden Delicious apple tree

Glossary

grafting—the process of inserting a stem with leaf buds into the stock of another tree; the process used by apple farmers to produce new apple trees

orchard—a planting of fruit trees, nut trees, or sugar maple trees

pollen—a powder made by flowers to help them create new seeds

pollination—the process of carrying pollen from the male part of a flower to the female part

sapling—a young tree that is taller than 6.6 feet (2 m) and has a trunk that is less than 4 inches (10 centimeters) around

seed—the part of a flower that will grow into a new plant

seedling—a young tree that is about 6 to 80 inches (15 to 200 cm) tall and has a trunk that is less than 4 inches (10 cm) around

stigma—the female part of the flower that makes seeds when pollinated

style—the long, thin part of a flower that holds the stigmas

23

To Learn More

More Books to Read

Ganeri, Anita. *From Seed to Apple*. Chicago: Heinemann Library, 2006.

Hibbert, Clare. *The Life of an Apple*. Chicago: Raintree, 2004.

Mayr, Diane. *Out and About at the Apple Orchard*. Minneapolis: Picture Window Books, 2003.

Tagliaferro, Linda. *The Life Cycle of an Apple Tree*. Mankato, Minn.: Capstone Press, 2007.

Taus-Bolstad, Stacy. *From Shoot to Apple*. Minneapolis: Lerner Publications Co., 2003.

On the Web

FactHound offers a safe, fun way to find educator-approved Internet sites related to this book.

Here's what you do:
1. Visit *www.facthound.com*
2. Chose your grade level.
3. Begin your search.

This book's ID number is 9781404851597

Index

Look for all of the books in the Amazing Science: Life Cycles series:

From Caterpillar to Butterfly: Following the Life Cycle
From Egg to Snake: Following the Life Cycle
From Mealworm to Beetle: Following the Life Cycle
From Pup to Rat: Following the Life Cycle
From Puppy to Dog: Following the Life Cycle
From Seed to Apple Tree: Following the Life Cycle
From Seed to Daisy: Following the Life Cycle
From Seed to Maple Tree: Following the Life Cycle
From Seed to Pine Tree: Following the Life Cycle
From Tadpole to Frog: Following the Life Cycle